SPIRIT BORNE

In an age of noise, it is good to be quiet. In an age of rush, it is good to stop. In an age of activity, it is good to meditate. Paul Bunday's book is a helpful way into using the Bible for contemplation. I found it very helpful.

Rob Frost

Many people in secular life and new age spiritualities are encouraging us to meditate. The Bible has been a resource for meditation for centuries. It is the richest and most profitable—it is the resource used by Jesus himself. These biblical meditations by Paul Bunday will provide a rich and edifying ingredient in anyone's prayer life.

**Canon David Gillett,
Principal, Trinity College, Bristol**

SPIRIT BORNE

An introduction to biblical meditation

Paul Bunday

The Bible Reading Fellowship
OPENING THE BIBLE

Text copyright © Paul Bunday 1993, 1996

The author asserts the moral right to be
identified as the author of this work.

Published by
The Bible Reading Fellowship
Peter's Way, Sandy Lane West
Oxford OX4 5HG
ISBN 0 7459 2976 1
Albatross Books Pty Ltd
PO Box 320, Sutherland
NSW 2232, Australia
ISBN 0 7324 0949 7

First edition 1996
10 9 8 7 6 5 4 3 2 1 0

Acknowledgments
Unless otherwise stated, scripture is
taken from The Revised Standard Version
of the Bible copyright © 1946, 1952, 1971
by the Division of Christian Education of the
National Council of the Churches of Christ
in the USA.

Extracts from the Authorized Version of the Bible
(AV), the rights of which are vested in the Crown,
are reproduced by permission of the Crown's
Patentee, Cambridge University Press.

Scripture marked (REB) is from the Revised English
Bible © 1989 by permission of Oxford and
Cambridge University Presses.

A catalogue record for this book is
available from the British Library

Printed and bound in Great Britain
by Cox and Wyman Ltd, Reading

Contents

*My warmest thanks to
Cynthia and Nancy for
their encouragement and
practical help in the
production of this book.*

Foreword

One of the greatest gifts which the Church has to make to the world is the gift of silence and guidance on how to use it. The gift will only be given by those who themselves are entering into the meaning of silence and are learning to meditate.

There is a huge literature concerned with this matter, much of it too specialized to be of use to the ordinary Christian disciple. The strength of this little book is that it does not emerge from a cloistered cell or an academic study, but from the pen of a man who has spent his ministry of nearly forty years in busy parishes. He has given us a spiritual book—well earthed.

Lord Coggan

First principles

When the business world starts promoting a spiritual technique there must be money in it. And meditation is a money-spinner these days because so many firms have found that working hours are lost through stress-related illnesses. Management feels that any technique which produces results can be used to prevent profits falling too sharply. Of course, some of these practices are far from Christian and so, in the long run, may produce more problems than they solve.

In the last fifteen or more years there has been a meditation boom. And I suppose I am part of it. My initial interest was caught in the late 1950s when I was beginning to develop a healing ministry in my church. Many of the leaders of the movement found meditation very helpful and so my interest was caught and held, but only in the area of healing. It was only about five years ago when my parochial ministry was passing through a period of frustration that I began to root the practice of meditation more deeply into daily devotional life.

I believe that there are three vital reasons for developing the practice of meditation.

The first and most important reason for engaging in meditation is that it focuses on the glory of God: it gives us a vision of his transcendence and immanence, which enables us to appreciate the reality of his nearness. He is the almighty, holy, living Lord. In meditation we give him our full attention, and we do it quietly, holding ourselves still, looking at him trustfully, reverently, knowing that he is looking at us compassionately. Everything else in life recedes. We are actually obeying the first commandment which is to hallow God's holy name. God himself is our central point of focus.

Almost certainly the act of meditation has begun with the sense of God there and I myself here. But it now needs to develop into something more profound. The sense of 'God there' and 'I here' needs to progress to the intimacy of what is sometimes called an 'I-Thou' relationship—indeed the expression of true relationship.

Secondly, we affirm that meditation is a deeply healing experience, as many are discovering, hence the interest of the commercial world. The whole of the human personality is involved. Because we have decided that it is important, or at least worth a try, we 'will' to engage in it, and so we make time and opportunity to practise it either by ourselves or in a group—ideally both. Our mind is involved because we hold, quietly and rationally, some particular word of truth in our thoughts. Here words of scripture are of the utmost importance so that we can ensure that it is God's truth that we are inwardly digesting. Our emotions are also involved, although not self-stimulated. In the quietness of the meditation, emotion may well be released because we are allowing the truth of God, focused in a prayer-phrase, to drop through our conscious minds down into our subconscious. Normally this will produce a sense of peace and well-being, a release of tension and stress, and may finally evolve into an experience of wholeness, or even holiness which, of course, are interconnected. God, the Holy Spirit, is touching us in body, mind and spirit therefore wholeness should be the natural result. We do not even need specifically to ask for it because to allow the truth of God to affect our mind and spirit is inevitably to experience wholeness.

Thirdly, and as important as the healing aspect of meditation, is the value that it has in making great Christian truths more personal, more part of us. Great preaching can do this but in a different way. The words of truth spoken by the preacher coupled with his own conviction and emotion can grip us in such a way that we enter into a new depth of understanding. However, in meditation we take great Christian truths and by revolving them around in our minds, chewing the cud on them as it were, we allow them to become more and more part of our experience. This is done quietly, with the body and emotions held as still as possible. It is certainly not mindless repetition in the hope that one day we shall really start believing what we are saying. Rather, it is taking a prayer phrase which we have received at an initial level of faith and, by warm welcome and quiet repetition, allowing the Holy Spirit to lead us to a deeper level of understanding. In this sense meditation is the process by which we give the Holy Spirit space to deepen his influence in our lives and to reprogramme our minds.

It is important to explain the true nature of meditation as so many people have the idea that it's a pious, subjective exercise that inadequate people undertake as an escape from reality. It is quite the reverse. It brings the glorious, transcendent reality of God into our experience in a remarkable way. It is a spiritual exercise that can benefit all Christians, and it may well be especially powerful for the many people today who are subject to stress. It also helps us to overcome the perennial problem of translating head knowledge into heart knowledge, of transforming the purely cerebral into the warmth of personal experience. As the classic devotional writers tell us, it enables us to possess our possessions in Christ and to become what we already truly are in him. So we can now move to some of the practical considerations which will help us to meditate creatively.

Practical points

You should be alone and quiet as you begin to meditate. Posture has some importance and the body should be comfortable. Your weight should be well spread over the chair so that there are no pressure points. There should be as near a right angle as is comfortable between the spine and the thighs. The body should be relaxed but the posture not sloppy, so that a deep stillness can begin to pervade you. If you are conscious of tension in your muscles, deliberately stretch and then relax them—feet, legs, arms, back and neck. A still body will help to bring about a still mind, but the former is easier to attain than the latter. The stillness is important so that the reality of God's presence can become the dominant experience. Perhaps the analogy to the formation of dew can be helpful. An unknown Christian has written:

Quietness and absorption bring the dew. At night, when the leaf and blade are still, the vegetable pores are open to receive the refreshing and invigorating bath; so spiritual dew comes from the quiet lingering in the Master's presence. Get still before him. Haste will prevent your receiving the dew. Wait before God until you feel saturated with his presence... Dew will never gather while there is either heat or wind; so the peace of God does not come forth to rest the soul until the STILL point is reached.

Here are some of the great secrets of meditation. There is the clear spiritual analogy from the natural phenomenon of dew formation with its encouragement to us to be still. There is also the injunction to 'wait before God' so that we give him room to move with blessing towards us. There are scores of biblical commands to 'wait for God' and also to 'wait on him'. The experience of waiting on God is at the heart of meditation. This is not the negative sort of waiting, such as waiting with mounting irritation for a train that is late when we have an important engagement which we shall miss. Waiting on God is totally positive and creative. He wants to take the initiative. And so we wait for him, look for him, hope for him and long for him.

I remember being given a verse of scripture by a well-wisher just before my institution to my first parish as rector. It was Psalm 27:14 and, in those days, I was mostly using the Authorized Version. I read:

Wait on the Lord: be of good courage, and he shall strengthen thine heart: wait, I say, on the Lord.

Immediately, I sensed that this was God's word to me and I was particularly struck by King David's use of '*I* say'. It made the statement so emphatic. It reinforced the command to wait in a dramatic way. And it was a word from the Lord that I particularly needed at that moment: I was very uptight about my new ministry. I'm prone to stress at the best of times but on this occasion I had been out of parochial ministry for six years while I served as a school chaplain so the future was unknown and rather threatening.

The experience of waiting on God was renewing and refreshing, just as the prophet Isaiah promised it would be when he said that 'they who wait for the Lord shall renew their strength, they shall mount up with wings like eagles, they shall run and not be weary, they shall walk and not faint' (Isaiah 40:31). From that moment I started to observe how often the Bible commands us to 'wait for God' or to 'wait on him'.

The chief point about the physical preparations for the act of meditation is that they are an aid to stillness of mind. There is nothing to be frightened of in stillness for it is a beautiful and creative experience. William Penn advised his children to: 'Love silence even in the mind; for thoughts are to that as words are to the body, troublesome; much speaking, as much thinking, spends. True silence is the rest of the mind; and is to the Spirit what sleep is to the body, nourishment and refreshment.'

And a poet has written:

O golden silence, bid our souls be still,
And on the foolish fretting of our care
Lay thy soft touch of healing unaware.

But for many of us true stillness comes very slowly and so the Psalmist's cry is so appropriate:

Be still before the Lord, and wait patiently for him.

PSALM 37:7

Meditation, then, requires patience, and patience involves spending time, trouble, effort and concentration. Unless you are prepared to give a minimum of fifteen minutes each day it would be best not to attempt it. You won't be taking it seriously enough to make any progress. It will be like dreaming of playing the piano without any practice times. Actually between twenty-five and thirty minutes daily is a more realistic period to give to meditation if you wish to make progress.

We have seen that physical posture has its place and time allocation is very important. Now I want to move to the matter of breathing which has revolutionized my own approach to meditation. Perhaps I should say at this point that there are a variety of different approaches to meditation and therefore I must not say that the breathing technique is necessarily vital for everyone. But it certainly is for myself. However, possibly it may not work in quite the same way for you, in which case keep experimenting until you discover the best way for yourself.

It was while reading a book about the Jesus Prayer that I first met the idea of linking breathing with prayer. Apparently some of the *staretz*, the Russian holy men, would use the Jesus Prayer continuously throughout the day, whatever else they were doing, by linking it to their breathing pattern. This enabled them, literally, to pray without ceasing.

The Jesus Prayer comes in different forms and I was attracted to the fullest one that I could find:

Lord Jesus Christ, Son of God, Saviour; have mercy on me a sinner.

I began experimenting with the breathing rhythm and eventually found one that suited me. Although it did not become a dominant part of my devotional life at that point, I never forgot it and drew on it from time to time.

About five years ago I began to incorporate the practice of meditation more fully into my daily devotional routine and, almost immediately, started to experiment with a breathing rhythm as I tried out various word patterns and prayer phrases to see which were most helpful and rewarding. I found that some meditations required a full in-and-out breath on each word, while with others two or three words could be used together on one breath. The meaning of the words often dictated the length of breath that was needed. By moving into a breathing rhythm a quiet balance was maintained, stress was markedly reduced and harmony of mind was enhanced. As the breathing became deeper, so the quiet repetition of the prayer phrase became slower. This was definitely beneficial and I can testify that the best results from meditation came when the prayer phrase was mentally repeated as slowly as possible. This gave practical confirmation of the truth expressed in the analogy of the dew—of the blessings of a quiet lingering in the Master's presence.

The Hebrew word for Spirit is *ruach*, which also means breath. The same word is also used for wind, and in meditation we are following, at the spiritual level, the example of the eagle: by setting the wings of faith at the critical angle, we are borne up by the Holy Spirit, lifted high by God's mighty power.

They who wait for the Lord... shall mount up with wings like eagles.

ISAIAH 40:31

Although there is no rule about it I have often found that the simpler the prayer phrase the more effective the meditation becomes. The use of monosyllables in the prayer phrase has a particular strength. Personally, I try to use the actual words of scripture or, at least, a meditation that is clearly based upon scripture. God has powerfully used the words of scripture in the lives of individuals. When we are using words in meditation with the specific intention that they should influence both our conscious and subconscious minds it is vital that we should only use words of proven truth and life. It is true that occasionally I change the word order of a biblical text when it is used as a prayer phrase. This is for two reasons: first, to enhance the regularity of the breathing rhythm; and secondly, to make the meditation more personal and therefore—hopefully—more powerful.

The breathing rhythm can be illustrated very simply in a phrase from Psalm 46:

Be still, and know that I am God.

PSALM 46:10

This requires a breath either in or out on every word and so the full in-and-out breathing pattern comes with every two words of the prayer phrase:

17

Be still—and know—that I—am God

This is a very helpful basic meditation which commands stillness in body and mind. It focuses on God himself: our minds are full of him. Although there is a split in the breathing at that point, we are actually using God's revealed name of 'I AM'. The prayer phrase has a harmonious balance to it. We can start at a natural speed of mental prayer and then, once the breathing rhythm is established, begin to slow down the prayer and correspondingly deepen the breathing.

Because our minds work pictorially, we are bound to discover unbidden thoughts and mental pictures arising within. Don't worry about them. Just continue the quiet repetition of the prayer phrase. We are not trying to stir up an emotional response, but we should not repress our emotions. Let them be quiet so that anything that is particularly experienced with heightened awareness is likely to originate in God himself. Our minds should be quiet but not inactive.

We become conscious of the meaning of the prayer phrase and of the rightness of remaining still in the awesome presence of our holy God. In the stillness we enjoy him for himself alone. The 'I-Thou' relationship is all that matters. We are giving God his true worth by focusing on him our full attention. And so, the meditation rises into worship and the worship becomes an offering— the offering of all that we know about ourselves to all that we know about God. This surely is the true end of meditation for it is not just some pious, subjective, interior exercise; not merely spiritual navel-gazing but true worship of the holy One, the Alpha and Omega, the source of all life and the ground of our being.

The only way to become proficient in meditation, as in anything else, is to practise it. The rest of this book will be the practical application of meditation as we share in a variety of prayer phrases. The heart of each meditation will be the use of a specific prayer phrase, but there will also be various suggestions for the centring-down process which comes first. This initial stage is meant to be a period when minds become quiet and so especially receptive to the use of the prayer phrase which follows.

Sometimes there can be a third and final stage which occurs as we emerge from the heart of meditation. Here we try to channel the meditation experience towards some part of life or human need by turning to intercession.

There will be three sections of meditations, each with its own distinctive character. First, meditations focused on the worship of God in and through Christ. Secondly, meditations which concentrate on wholeness and healing. Lastly, a variety of meditations where we seek to deepen our understanding and experience of some great Christian truth. In other words, we turn head knowledge into heart knowledge.

Meditations focused on the worship of God

First, we need to learn to wait for God and to wait on God in worship. We have already spoken about this. Here are some of the many Old Testament verses which tell us to 'wait':

Be still before the Lord, and wait patiently for him.

PSALM 37:7

Wait for the Lord, and keep to his way, and he will exalt you to possess the land.

PSALM 37:34

I wait for the Lord, my soul waits, and in his word I hope.

PSALM 130:5

Lead me in thy truth, and teach me, for thou art the God of my salvation; for thee I wait all the day long.

PSALM 25:5

Therefore the Lord waits to be gracious to you; therefore he exalts himself to show mercy to you... blessed are all those who wait for him.

ISAIAH 30:18

Those who wait for the Lord shall possess the land.

PSALM 37:9

Waiting for God implies that we are hoping for him to act, but in his way and in his time. There is no sense of stress or impatience. We are resting in him, trusting in him, placing our full weight upon him.

Wait

So let's look at the first text and turn it into a meditation. The breathing is straightforward, in and out on each pair of syllables except for the word 'patiently'—here we will need to lengthen the breath slightly, because of the extra syllable. This will effectively emphasize the word.

> Be still—before—the Lord—
> and wait—patiently—for him

Now take this verse and spiritually 'chew the cud' on it. Quietly revolve it round and round your mind for at least fifteen minutes. In the later stages of the meditation you may find it helpful to substitute for the word 'patiently' some other adverb such as 'hopefully', 'trustfully', 'expectantly', 'thankfully'. This is not so much changing the basic meaning of the prayer phrase as filling it out with the truth that is already, implicitly, there. In meditation the mind is attentive but not stretched; quietly concentrated on the prayer phrase but not stressed.

Normally, you will be sitting comfortably but with reverent attention. However, it is sometimes helpful to revolve the prayer phrase around your mind while you are walking, washing up or gardening. Occasionally you may fall asleep in your normal sitting posture. It is best not to worry about this. Probably you have gone to sleep in the Spirit and will find it especially refreshing. However, if you start falling asleep too regularly during meditation try a harder chair.

Wait for the Lord; be strong and brave, and put your hope in the Lord.

PSALM 27:14 (REB)

The Revised English Bible translation of Psalm 27:14 had an important bearing on my New Forest ministry. During that period I remember an interesting experience of waiting that came my way. I had never seen badgers in the wild although there were many badger sets to be found in the New Forest. I had noted one with many signs of recent working near a pleasant stretch of water called Eyworth Pond. I set out one summer's evening with my elder son and moved into position well downwind from the sets long before dusk. We then sat in silence and waited. It was a beautiful evening and our quietness allowed the usual forest wildlife to move about, around and on the pond. We waited and waited until we could no longer see the sets. There was no sign of the badgers, but it certainly wasn't a wasted evening. The waiting had proved truly beneficial and I returned home more deeply at peace than I had been for weeks.

And now we turn to the meditation. Every word is a monosyllable which is a great advantage when we move into the breathing rhythm. There is an 'in' and 'out' breath for each pair of words. The only slightly difficult part is the ending, where a full breath is needed on 'in the Lord'.

Wait for—the Lord—
be strong—and brave—
and put—your hope—in the Lord

Meditation on the Trinity

This meditation takes us to the heart of Christian faith and experience. It is the true basis of all spiritual growth. In it there is not only the adoration of a Trinity of persons in the one Godhead but the meditation itself is arranged in a trinity of words and lines.

First then, the meditation on God:

Wait on God.

This is the starting point. Invest in the single word 'wait' all that we have already experienced of its meaning in meditation. Focus on God himself, the almighty, the omniscient, the omnipresent. Secondly, we move on to the specially revealed character of God in the Old Testament as the one who is Other, and who is 'of purer eyes than to behold evil' (Habakkuk 1:13). He is the holy One, before whom even the highest angelic orders veil their faces. We now recognize this as we say:

Holy, holy, Lord.

Now with these two phrases as the backcloth to the meditation we move to the most wonderful truth revealed in the New Testament. Jesus himself has encouraged us to address this almighty, all-knowing, ever present, holy God as Father, indeed Father in the most intimate sense: 'Abba, Father'. And so the third line of the prayer phrase becomes:

Abba, Father, God.

The meaning of these words is so profound that it is imperative that we give a full breath to each word. As we breathe them in awe, reverence, wonder, love and praise lengthen the breath to the fullest extent. We are in the holy of holies and can never say them too slowly:

Wait—on—God
Holy—holy—Lord
Abba—Father—God

We now move to the meditation on the Son, and here again we shall be using words that seem so simple and yet which have such a profound meaning that pages could be written about them. The first phrase is:

Rest in Christ.

The word 'rest' here is a kind of shorthand which sums up all of our Lord Jesus Christ's mighty acts. Its meaning begins in the incarnation, the Son of God living a human life in its fulness. It continues in the suffering and victory of Calvary's cross where Jesus made a full act of atonement. This was announced and validated in his resurrection and made final and complete in his ascension. The word 'rest', then, refers to our response to the Son's completed work of salvation. We rest in it because it is totally, completely and wonderfully finished. We can add nothing to it, but we can accept it, receive it and rest our faith upon it. Thus, we don't use the word lightly. It contains within it a fulness of meaning and a wealth of grace. It sums up all that Jesus has done for us and affirms that we have received it most thankfully.

We come, then, to the next two lines of the prayer phrase and move straight to Jesus' own words in John 15 where he affirms that he is the vine and we are the branches and that the secret of life for the Christian is to dwell in him, so that he can dwell in us. There is to be no stress or strain about this. Just as the life-giving sap flows from the parent stem into the spreading branches producing foliage and fruit so, by analogy, the life of Christ flows into and out from all who are united with him by faith.

Dwell in him.

We dwell in him who is our righteousness, our redemption, our wisdom, our holiness, our way, our truth and our life. And he dwells in us so that his life may flow out into the world. Different versions of the Bible use variations of translation at this point. The AV has the beautiful word 'abide'—we are to 'abide in Christ and he in us'. Other versions use 'live', 'dwell' or 'remain'. In the prayer phrase here I have used the monosyllable 'dwell', but the other words are equally good.

Thus the second part of this Trinitarian meditation becomes:

Rest—in—Christ
Dwell—in—him
He—in—us

Again, there is a full breath on each word.

The meditation on the Holy Spirit starts in the Old Testament and then moves on to John 15. We remember the words of Jesus that 'apart from me you can do nothing' (John 15:5) and look back to the prophet Zechariah's declaration: 'Not by might, nor by power, but by my Spirit, says the Lord' (Zechariah 4:6). Only the Holy Spirit can continue Jesus' ministry in the world effectively. Only the Holy Spirit is our true power and inspiration in life.

The second phrase also has its origin in the Last Supper teaching where Jesus speaks about how the Paraclete is going to replace him. In speaking about the Holy Spirit here Jesus uses a word rich in meaning, for Paraclete can be translated counsellor, adviser, defender at law, friend, helper or guide. We now pick up that word in the meditation and then finally end with an invocation to the Holy Spirit to continue his ministry in and through us.

Until now each prayer phrase has been an act

of affirmation or adoration. But now—for the only time in the meditation—we use intercession. There is, in fact, no ending to the prayer, 'Come Holy Spirit.' The cry takes its meaning from everything that has gone before in the meditation, but now we project it outwards into every circumstance of life and every part of the world's need:

> Not—by—might
> Par—a—clete
> Come—Holy—Spirit

This meditation can be used in three quite separate parts or these can be combined to make one full Trinitarian devotional exercise. The full meditation becomes:

> Wait—on—God
> Holy—holy—Lord
> Abba—Father—God
>
> Rest—in—Christ
> Dwell—in—him
> He—in—us
>
> Not—by—might
> Par—a—clete
> Come—Holy—Spirit

As we become familiar with this meditation there is an important change that may be made so that the words can become more personal. In the second section which concerns the meditation on the Son, allow the second and third lines to change into the first person singular, which then become:

Rest in Christ
I in him
He in me

There comes a point where this change is entirely natural and so there is no need to rush into it. Let it evolve just when you are ready for it. But when it happens, catch your breath in wonder.

The Jesus Prayer

In this first section of meditations of worship we come now to the Jesus Prayer. Although the last part of this powerful meditation is intercession, the first part is affirmation and adoration. It can be used in slightly different forms. Its briefest statement is:

Jesus, Son of God, have mercy on me.

Personally I prefer to use the longer form which is:

Lord Jesus Christ, Son of God, Saviour; have mercy on me, a sinner.

When I first met the Jesus Prayer I could not understand why it had won such a powerful place in Christian devotion. It seemed so brief and almost stated the obvious. But like many great masterpieces it yielded its secret slowly. I gradually came to see that every word carried a profound weight of meaning so that in addition to being a prayer and a meditation it was also an affirmation of faith. As we move through it we pause at every word.

Let's remember that we are engaged in meditation and so we are using this phrase devotionally. That does not mean to say that we ignore the theological meaning. We can't use it at all if it's theologically incorrect, but we are not using the Jesus Prayer as if we were reciting the Nicene Creed. May I suggest that you use the words of the Jesus Prayer in your meditation by investing them with the deepest meaning of which you are capable. In this way we don't have to define exactly whether we are bringing an orthodox, neo-orthodox, conservative, liberal, radical or revisionist interpretation to them.

Lord: right at the beginning we invoke the divine name. We breathe it with reverence. Yahweh, the one who says, 'I am who I am' and 'I will become what I will become' (Exodus 3:14). The flames of the burning bush still protect that name as truly holy.

Jesus: the incarnate Word of God. The one who laid aside every one of the garments of divinity and was born as a baby, shared our life at every point: child, teenager, adult—totally human. Jesus, one of the most common first names of his day, a diminutive form of Joshua. We call on Jesus, the man for others, our brother who identified in every possible way with us.

Christ: Jesus is the Christ, the anointed one, the Messiah. He is anchored in history. The whole of the Old Testament is a preparation for his ministry. He comes as the fulfilment of God's purpose uniquely revealed in scripture. The life of Jesus can only be given its true meaning when it is interpreted against the backcloth of the Old Testament. Its pages alone define who Jesus was, why he came and what his life meant. Some people think of the word 'Christ' as Jesus' surname. In one profound way they are right, for it defines Jesus' family background.

Son of God: this phrase perfectly balances 'Jesus Christ'. Jesus, the Son of God, is the second person of the Trinity.

Saviour: its beauty and power carry their own interpretation for us. No doubt all Christians unite in viewing Jesus as the perfect mediator, making full atonement for us, but in that way which we personally find most helpful and moving. God was in Christ reconciling the world to himself (2 Corinthians 5:19) and so Jesus has made peace for us by the blood of his cross (Colossians 1:20).

Have mercy on me a sinner: and so this final part of the meditation is a prayer—a response to all that has gone before. It is truly personal as it concerns the most profound aspect of our relationship to God. Everything comes to us by God's grace, and his mercy is the complement of his grace. Grace means that God is giving us that which we don't deserve. And mercy means that God is not giving us what we do deserve. And, incidentally, peace comes to us when we receive and live in God's grace and mercy. Since the practice of meditation is meant to lead us deeply into the peace of God which passes all understanding, we can never emphasize enough that it must be based on an understanding and experience of God's grace and mercy.

We are sinners because we fall short in every part of natural human life: wills, minds, emotions, relationships, imaginations are all twisted and warped from God's original perfection. Our lives are self-centred rather than God-centred. To change the picture for a moment, we acknowledge here that the infection of sin has dis-eased every area of life. But God is a God of mercy and grace and we now rejoice in his salvation, reconciliation and healing in Christ.

Finally, a word about the breathing rhythm. This is slightly more complicated than usual. I suggest a full breath on each of the first three words. Then a full breath on each of the next two phrases, followed by a breath on each of the last three pairs of words:

> **Lord—Jesus—Christ**
> **Son of God—Saviour**
> **Have mercy—on me—a sinner**

Meditations on healing and wholeness

By his stripes we are healed

At the beginning of this second section of meditations we move straight to the epicentre of the healing ministry of Jesus, which, St Matthew affirms (8:17), was the cross of Calvary for he actually quotes Isaiah 53:4 to explain the source of the healing—'He took our infirmities and bore our diseases.' As Isaiah goes on to say: 'By his stripes we are healed' (Isaiah 53:5). This is the foundation for our healing meditations.

So that these, and other meditations, may enable the Holy Spirit to release his full power within us, we need to practise the principle of centring down before we move into the use of the actual meditation prayer phrase. This centring-down process should bring a calmness and stillness to the body and mind so that our spirits are truly receptive and tuned in to God's Spirit during the twenty or so minutes of the main meditation.

Here the first stage of centring down is to read through Isaiah 53, very slowly, so that the prayer phrase is used in context. As we do so we can marvel how the fourth and final 'suffering servant' prophecy was so wonderfully fulfilled in Jesus.

By his stripes we are healed.

Then we could use two other passages, one from the twentieth century and the other written 300 years earlier, to help us prepare for the full meditation experience. First, Dr Frank Lake, who was a missionary doctor before returning home and founding the Clinical Theology movement, wrote about the cross:

Christ's own being on the cross contained all the clashing contrarieties and scandalous fates of human existence. Life himself was identified with death; the light of the world was enveloped in darkness. The feet of the man who said, 'I am the way', feared to tread upon it and prayed, 'If it is possible, not that way'. The water of life was thirsty. The bread of life was hungry. The divine lawgiver was himself unjustly outlawed. The holy one was identified with the unholy. The lion of Judah was crucified as a lamb. The hands that made the world and raised the dead

*were fixed with nails until they were rigid in
death. Men's hope of heaven descended in hell.
He was deprived of all his rights, to be with us
in our privation. He accepted this 'contradiction'
of sinners against himself. He bore the ultimate
deprivation of dereliction.*

Frank Lake, by permission of Clinical Theology Association

And secondly, the words of a seventeenth-
century hymn, sometimes attributed to St
Francis Xavier, one of the greatest Christian
missionaries:

*My God I love thee; not because
I hope for heaven thereby,
Nor yet because who love thee not
Are lost eternally.*

*Thou, O my Jesus, thou did'st me
Upon the cross embrace;
For me did'st bear the nails and spear,
And manifold disgrace.*

*And griefs and torments numberless,
And sweat of agony;
Yea, death itself; and all for me
Who was thine enemy.*

*Then why, O blessed Jesu Christ,
Should I not love thee well?
Not for the sake of winning heaven,
Nor of escaping hell;*

Not from the hope of gaining aught,
Nor seeking a reward;
But as thy self hast lovéd me,
O ever-loving Lord.

So would I love thee, dearest Lord,
And in thy praise will sing;
Solely because thou art my God,
And my most loving King.

Seventeenth century, translated by E. Caswall

By his stripes we are healed.

That is the pure objective statement of truth. But now, as we revolve the prayer phrase round and round in our minds, we can allow the meaning to deepen and become more personal. Let's now hear the Lord actually addressing us from the cross so that the prayer phrase becomes:

By my stripes you are healed.

This allows us, in turn, to appropriate the divine healing and wholeness which flows from the cross by affirming:

By your stripes we are healed.

And then the final stage becomes the most personal of all:

By your stripes I am healed.

The breathing pattern is straightforward using a full breath for each word.

By—your—stripes—I—am—healed

There can be no more profound meditation than this as we enter the experience of wholeness. Like the Jesus Prayer we can use it, not only in the specific meditation times but throughout the day, frequently returning to it so that it saturates our subconscious mind with the healing that constantly radiates out from the cross.

Wash me, Lord

We are created to be whole people. The physical, emotional and spiritual parts of our human nature are so blended that they should be one united whole. This means that the physical, emotional, mental and spiritual dimensions are constantly interacting with each part. Dis-ease in one affects all. Healing in one part influences the other parts of life towards wholeness. Therefore one of the most important impulses towards wholeness of life comes when we seek the healing of our spirits through the forgiveness and cleansing which God alone can impart. This meditation is intended to make this experience profound and life-enhancing, and it is focused on the supper table where Jesus begins to wash his disciples' feet.

First, however, as we start to centre down, we could use a prayer by John V. Taylor, former Bishop of Winchester. This starts an awakening process so that the Holy Spirit can convict us of our need of cleansing and then lead us to experience God's wonderful provision for that need. It's a prayer which moves us outside our narrow introverted circle of personal guilt and helps us to see the corporate sin of which we are part.

We confess to you, Lord, the discord of our
  world,
to which we contribute and in which we share.
We confess the fearful needs of mankind,
before which we stand inactive and indifferent.
Forgive us Christians for being so unsure of our
  Good News
and so unready to tell it.
Awaken our imagination to be your voice in us,
Deepen our understanding of the way of the Cross,
Embolden our obedience to your will for our
  world
Through the power of Jesus Christ our Lord.

Now we move to the first verse of a much-loved poem which later became a hymn:

Dear Lord and Father of mankind,
Forgive our foolish ways
Reclothe us in our rightful mind,
In purer lives thy service find,
In deeper reverence, praise.

                                        J.G. Whittier

Once again we're coming to *Abba*, Father. When we're confident of an understanding and welcoming acceptance we are not so fearful about unburdening ourselves and laying bare the darker secrets of moral failure and inner guilt.

We ask for forgiveness for our 'foolish ways'. That seemingly almost innocuous phrase carries the moral punch of a world heavyweight fighter. It certainly doesn't mean mild moral aberrations or sloppy selfishness. It goes to the heart of the diagnosis of human sinfulness which Jesus made when he said that anyone who called his brother 'you fool' (Matthew 5:22) would be in danger of hell fire. The word he used means a person totally devoid of moral sensitivity or understanding, someone whose concept of right and wrong has become turned upside-down. It's a word deliberately meant to stop us in our tracks and to pose the awesome question, 'Could this be true of me?' So forgiveness needs to become a reality in order that we can have a mind reclothed and remade from the inside.

Then seeing clearly and thinking sensitively we can find that perfect balance of both the reverent praise of a living God and the holy life which expresses itself in joyful service.

Now we come to the meditation itself. There are three lines of three words each; and all but one are monosyllables. Nothing could be simpler but some of the words carry a profound depth of spiritual meaning, rather like the word 'rest' which we discussed earlier. We join the disciples at the supper table and, as Peter did, suddenly see what Jesus is saying about the need of being washed. Our centring-down preparation has led us to this point. So, with Peter, we cry:

Wash me Lord.

Again, like Peter, we realize that we need washing in every part of life. When one of the Anglican 'Articles of Religion' says that we are 'very far gone from original righteousness', it means that the infection of sin has penetrated every area of our being—our wills, minds, emotions, imaginations, words and deeds. We need that total washing that Peter suddenly recognized that he needed. And so the second line of the meditation is:

Feet, heart, head.

Perhaps I should clarify that I'm using the word 'heart' here in its modern rather than biblical sense. I'm thinking of it as the seat of our emotions. So it's as though we are working our way up from the physical problems represented by feet, through the distorted world of the emotions to the final source of motivation in the mind, imagination and the will—the place where we choose for good or evil, where we give our consent to sin. This may sound harsh, but it echoes Jesus' own words about the place of choosing—what the Bible calls the 'heart':

Wicked thoughts, murder, adultery, fornication, theft, perjury, slander—these all proceed from the heart.
                              MATTHEW 15:19 (REB)

And now we move to the solution of the problem, the place where God answers our cry for help. In our weakness and confusion, guilt and helplessness, 'stung by the scorpion sin' as Charles Wesley wrote, God now provides the antidote:

Water, blood, fire.

The disciples felt the cool water and the gentle massage of Jesus' firm hands as he physically refreshed tired feet. The healing began at that moment. But now the cleansing moves inside our lives, and the 'blood of Jesus his Son [which] cleanses us from all sin' (1 John 1:7) is applied to disordered minds and spirits. The washing is now within our lives. The agonized cry of King David as he wrestled with the guilt of murder and adultery, 'Purge me with hyssop, and I shall be clean' (Psalm 51:7), is now answered by the atoning blood of Jesus Christ proclaiming peace, reconciliation, forgiveness and wholeness. The purifying process is made doubly secure by the fire of the Holy Spirit as he cleanses every part of life, just as impure gold is refined in a furnace. 'He is like a refiner's fire' (Malachi 3:2) is a prophecy of the work of the Holy Spirit as God wills that we should be changed and remade in Christ's likeness.

Finish then thy new creation,
Pure and spotless let us be:
Let us see thy great salvation,
Perfectly restored in thee.
Changed from glory into glory,
Till in heaven we take our place;
Till we cast our crowns before thee,
Lost in wonder, love and praise.

Charles Wesley

Both the cleansing blood of Christ and the purifying work of the Holy Spirit are really experienced at the same time. The order of the words in the phrase does not imply a similar order in experience.

The breathing rhythm, again, is straight-forward, with a full breath on each word:

Wash—me—Lord
Feet—heart—head
Water—blood—fire

There is just one addition that can be made if we wish to strengthen the sense of personal conviction of sin. Jesus, himself, affirmed that the Holy Spirit's ministry is to convict of sin, righteousness and judgment (John 16:8). Perhaps we feel that these words are heavy and threatening, yet they are intended to lead us to life. We have a natural reluctance to visit the doctor when we sense something is wrong. But the purpose of going is to bring us to health. Our doctor can only diagnose disease if it is actually there and then the sooner it is diagnosed the better. The Holy Spirit can only convict of sin when there is actually something wrong with our lives. And then he immediately points us to the remedy which will bring salvation-wholeness.

And so this phrase can be inserted at the beginning of the meditation if required: 'He will convict of sin, righteousness and judgment.'

I am the Lord who makes you whole

This meditation is based on God's revelation in Exodus that he is a healing God.

I am the Lord that healeth thee.

EXODUS 15:26 (AV)

This truth keeps rising to the surface in prophetic ministry, principally in the time of Elisha. But, of course, it's Jesus' ministry of healing which brings it to centre stage. No one who came to Jesus with a problem which needed a compassionate response was ever turned away. The only failure he ever experienced was in his own home town of Nazareth, where his healing ministry was not accepted and those with whom he had grown up would not come to him. How his heart must have ached. People whom he knew so well, old school friends, neighbours, relatives of Joseph and Mary were just too familiar with him. How could the carpenter do these things? But in the words of his great promise, all who truly came to him would never be cast out. And so lepers came, the blind and the deaf, the lame and the paralysed, those with mental illnesses—and he healed them all. Such was the resurrection power that flowed through him that even the dead were raised. Jairus's daughter was lifted by hand and word of command out of the sleep of death. The funeral cortège of the widow's son was halted at the last moment and the mother's black despair turned to joy. The four-days-dead Lazarus, with his decaying body, was brought to life with the echoing command, 'Lazarus, come out!'

Jesus, in his healing ministry, was incarnating—living out in a human life—the very heart of God as he suffered with his hurt creation. It was as though the rays of the divine light of God's love were caught in the lens of Jesus' mind and then focused on one suffering person after another, just as the magnifying glass concentrates the rays of the sun to a focal point of burning intensity. Time and again the record is given, 'immediately he was made well' (see Mark 1:31; 2:12; 5:29, 42; John 4:53). And yet we recognize that the intention of Jesus was always to go further than the mere restoration of physical health. He wanted everyone to be truly whole, to be totally unified and harmonized in body, mind and spirit. He wanted us all to be holy and to experience full salvation.

This meditation, then, is of profound importance: so simple and yet so far reaching in its implications and possibilities. If we used no other each day we would be opening our lives in such a way that the love and light of God could radiate into all the dark corners of the conscious and subconscious mind, where we still need healing before we can become truly whole personalities. And, of course, many of us will immediately recognize particular areas of life where our need of healing is all too obvious.

So that we may use this prayer phrase to the full, the centring-down process is especially important. Perhaps you would like to start with a very simple healing meditation that can actually be used by itself, divorced from any other devotional exercise if you wish. The words are a slightly amended form of a verse from Whittier's great hymn:

Immortal love, for ever full,
For ever flowing free,
For ever shared, for ever whole,
A never ebbing sea!

The biblical background is the story of the woman who had suffered from a haemorrhage for twelve years but believed that she would be cured if she could just touch the edge of Jesus' clothing. Her problem was that, being ceremonially unclean, she should not have been in a crowded street to start with. Added to which, in her weakened condition, she would have had great difficulty in forcing herself through the mass of people to get near enough to Jesus to touch him. Her desperation and her faith provided the answer and she found healing as she reached out to him.

In meditation we sometimes have to press

through a milling crowd of unruly emotions and cross eddying currents of stress. Sometimes physical or psychological illness seems to place an almost insuperable barrier between ourselves and the presence of Christ. Whittier's words will help us to reach the point where we can start to use the prayer phrase:

The healing of your seamless dress
Is by our beds of pain;
We touch you in life's throng and press,
And we are whole again.

Repeat them as slowly, quietly and purposefully as possible. Allow the Holy Spirit to apply the Gospel incident behind the verse to your own situation whatever the pressing, crowded difficulties you may be experiencing.

We can now move forward to use the prayer phrase. The breathing rhythm is straightforward.

I am—the Lord—who makes—you whole

During the period of silent repetition of the prayer phrase, some practical application of it may become clear. Focus the healing presence of Jesus Christ on someone known to you who is ill. Radiate his wholeness into the sick person's life, particularly in those areas where the major problem lies. Accompany them through all the personal difficulties which surround them at the moment so that they too may touch the hem of his garment. Picture it happening and hear his words to them, as you have heard them for yourself: 'I am the Lord who makes you whole.'

These words could also be used to conclude many of the other meditations in this book.

Peace, be still

This meditation takes the story of Jesus stilling
the storm on the sea of Galilee and universalizes
it into our own experience. As we reflect back on
the original story we need first to catch the panic
or fear of the disciples. It must have been an
unusually severe squall for some of those in the
boat were experienced fishermen who had
worked that stretch of water since leaving the
synagogue school. However, such storms could
blow up very quickly as the wind funnelled onto
the sea from the mountains of Moab. We also
need to note the utter exhaustion of Jesus
following a day of pressurized activity as he
taught the crowds and healed those who came to
him. The change of motion in the boat, the rising
wind, the soaking spray and the hysterical voices
of the crew did not wake him. Only the rough
hand on his shoulder and the cry, 'Master, we're
sinking', bought him to consciousness.

From deep sleep Jesus moved to authoritative
control in a matter of seconds. He took in the
situation and addressed the chaotic and
threatening sea with the decisive words of
command, 'Peace, be still.' The water recognized
its creator's voice and obeyed. Jesus was indeed

Lord of that situation and the result was 'a great calm'. All was at peace (Mark 4:39).

As we move through this meditation we shall need to bring our own personal circumstances into focus and superimpose the biblical incident over them. The disciples were in a situation that they could not control. They felt helpless and fearful. They had no personal solution to their problem. Are we in like case? Where do we feel that life is out of control and that we have no personal answers to problems that confront us? So we, like the disciples, come to Jesus and say: 'Save us, Lord' (Matthew 8:25, REB).

We must now allow Jesus to reproduce his action in our lives. He must take control of the situation. His appraisal of our problem is complete and we now need to hear his word of authority, 'Peace, be still', as he brings his controlling power to bear on our problem. He does this because he is Lord, the risen, reigning Lord of the universe, before whom every knee must bow. And so as his reigning authority is exercised there is 'a great calm'. In this meditation we affirm that however great our problem, Jesus is greater. Perhaps we find it difficult to identify exactly what we mean or even to understand what we mean at this point. But we can at least define our problem well enough—it looms so threateningly over us. The power of the meditation is that we are affirming that Jesus is greater.

And so to the meditation itself. As you centre down, read the Gospel story. Use your imagination to put yourself in the boat with Jesus. You know the lake well—it is where you work each day, and you have seen squalls before. But now even you are alarmed. Things are out of your control. But with a word Jesus takes command of your external and internal anxieties. As he says 'Peace, be still', you know deep calm.

That day, in the evening, he said to them, 'Let us cross over to the other side of the lake.' So they left the crowd and took him with them in the boat in which he had been sitting; and some other boats went with him. A fierce squall blew up and the waves broke over the boat until it was all but swamped. Now he was in the stern asleep on a cushion; they roused him and said, 'Teacher, we are sinking! Do you not care?' He awoke and rebuked the wind, and said to the sea, 'Silence! Be still!' The wind dropped and there was a dead calm. He said to them, 'Why are you such cowards? Have you no faith even now?' They were awestruck and said to one another, 'Who can this be? Even the wind and the sea obey him.'

MARK 4:35–41 (REB)

The prayer phrase which picks out the salient features of the incident is in four lines of three words each. Almost all are monosyllables and so the full breath comes on each word:

Save—us—Lord
Peace—be—still
Jesus—is—Lord
All—is—calm

God's perfect peace

Thou dost keep him in perfect peace, whose mind is stayed on thee, because he trusts in thee.

ISAIAH 26:3

The word 'peace' in the English language is beautiful but in Hebrew it contains a greater wealth of meaning. *Shalom* implies a complete harmony of life, a unified wholeness of well-being. It is a state of total reconciliation between us and God, between all people in their relationships and between us and our created environment. Of course, the New Testament makes it quite clear that we can never know the peace of God until first we have peace with God. This only comes through faith, in response to Jesus Christ who himself is our peace. His cross is the place where we witness the great peace treaty that God has sealed in his blood. And so, from this point, the presence of the Holy Spirit becomes a reality, and one of the principal fruits of his presence is divine peace.

In this meditation we shall live in the peace of God so that our own minds may be saturated with his presence. The prayer phrase is a promise with a condition. God's peace is promised to us when our minds are stayed on him. Being 'stayed' on God means the same as 'abiding in Christ' which we have already discussed. All life revolves round him. He is the focal point. Although, at first, we are making him the chief object of our attention, the perspective gradually changes and he becomes the subject and we are then the object. I remember one great twentieth-century preacher, Martin Lloyd-Jones who would never give television interviews on the grounds that it was impossible to discuss God impersonally in a studio as an object to be examined—he must always be the subject of life.

The final phrase of the meditation reinforces the need to be in a trustful relationship with God if we desire his perfect peace. We have been examining the prayer phrases that are revolved around the mind in meditation and we may be in danger of neglecting the need for personal trust in him—to know him as the source of life and then to receive his perfect peace, his *shalom*.

As we centre down for this meditation we use the words of an old hymn which moves us through many of life's most disturbing experiences. The question marks in all but the last verse are vitally important. How is peace possible amidst the evil, fear and horror of the world? Where is peace to be found when life is full of stress and pressure? How can one be calm when personal sorrow is breaking our heart or we are stretched with anxiety over an absence? Where is peace to be found when the future is full of uncertainty and clearly threatening? Each fundamental question is posed—and then answered.

> Peace, perfect peace, in this dark world of
> sin?
> The blood of Jesus whispers peace within.
>
> Peace, perfect peace, by thronging duties
> press'd?
> To do the will of Jesus, this is rest.
>
> Peace, perfect peace, with sorrows surging
> round?
> On Jesus' bosom nought but calm is found.
>
> Peace, perfect peace, with loved ones far
> away?
> In Jesus' keeping we are safe and they.
>
> Peace, perfect peace, our future all unknown?
> Jesus we know, and He is on the throne.
>
> Peace, perfect peace, death shadowing us and
> ours?
> Jesus has vanquish'd death and all its
> powers.
>
> It is enough: earth's struggles soon shall
> cease,
> And Jesus calls to heav'ns perfect peace.

E.H. Bickersteth

The breathing rhythm is a little more complicated here and I suggest the full breaths as follows:

You—will keep him—in per—fect peace—
whose mind—is stayed—on you—
because—he trusts—in you

The meditation can be made even more personal by changing the pronouns slightly:

You will keep me in perfect peace, my mind is stayed on you, because I trust in you.

There is a particularly appropriate post-meditation prayer at this point. It is known as the Prayer of St Francis:

Lord, make me a channel of your peace,
That where there is hatred—I may bring love,
That where there is wrong—
I may bring the spirit of forgiveness,
That where there is discord—I may bring
  harmony,
That where there is error—I may bring truth,
That where there is doubt—I may bring faith,
That where there is despair—I may bring
  hope,
That where there are shadows—I may bring
  light,
That where there is sadness—I may bring joy.

Lord, grant that I may seek
Rather to comfort—than be comforted;

To understand—than to be understood;
To love—than to be loved;
For it is by giving—that one receives;
It is by self forgetting—that one finds;
It is by forgiving—that one is forgiven;
It is by dying—that one awakens to eternal
   life.

Sunbathing in God's healing light

During my theological training in the mid 1950s a London vicar spoke to us about his parochial ministry of healing. He must have been one of the pioneers of that particular ministry in those days. He described an incident when he was called into a psychiatric hospital to see a patient in a padded cell. The hospital authorities had been unable to cope with the man's violent outbursts and the vicar was their last resort. He entered the cell and found it quite impossible to make any contact with the man. So he sat down on the floor and began to repeat over and over the words of a healing meditation. He spoke softly, almost to himself, but just audibly enough for the severely disturbed man to hear. The words that he used were:

I am sunbathing in God's healing light.

He repeated these words slowly for almost half an hour. Nothing else was spoken, just the continuous quiet revolving of the prayer phrase. Very gradually the patient calmed down. He then grew attentive to the words and then, finally, a real conversation resulted.

As we use these words as a healing meditation, you may well find difficulty in introducing a breathing rhythm. On this occasion it may be best to ignore it and concentrate purely on the words of the meditation. If you find a pattern emerging which suits you, this will be a bonus.

The centring-down exercise for this meditation involves using the imagination to the full for we are allowing God's light to focus on ourselves. At the beginning of creation God said, 'Let there be light' (Genesis 1:3) and created light appeared. But behind the created light there is God who is light. 'God is light' affirms St John (1 John 1:5), and Jesus personified that revelation in his own life when he stated, 'I am the light of the world' (John 8:12).

We all know the properties of a magnifying glass. It focuses the sun's rays so that a point of intense light and heat results. Jesus himself focused the healing rays of God's light upon many needy people in his ministry through his own inner life of faith and love. In this meditation we are focusing the continuous rays of God's light upon ourselves. And then, at the post-meditation stage, we can focus them on others who have needs of healing and wholeness.

Just as the lens needs to be held still if the sun's rays are to be focused accurately, so we become still and recognize that God's light is always shining upon us and that spiritual sunbathing is a deeply healing experience.

Meditations that deepen faith and experience

Lastly, we come to the third and largest section of meditations which are used to deepen Christian faith and experience. We begin at the most profound level of Christian revelation which says that everything we are and have comes from the God of all grace.

My grace is sufficient

It has been said that all true religion begins in grace and ends in gratitude. No other two words sum up the Christian faith more completely. Time and time again in St Paul's letters we have the thudding refrain, 'By grace... by grace... by grace'. And so, appropriately, the first meditation in this third section is from St Paul (my translation).

My grace is all you need: my power perfected in weakness.

2 CORINTHIANS 12:9

Before we move to the meditation proper our centring down is particularly concerned with considering the meaning of grace. Grace is God's love coming to undeserving people in a totally unexpected way. By definition it will always be astonishing, amazing and unexpected. It wouldn't be grace otherwise. 'Only when grace is recognised to be incomprehensible is it grace,' says Karl Barth. And so it has a quality that is finally beyond definition. W.H. Griffith Thomas, one-time Principal of Wycliffe Hall, Oxford, takes us to the heart of the matter:

Grace means more, far more than we can put into words, because it means nothing less than the infinite character of God himself. It includes mercy for the undeserving and unmerciful, help for the helpless and hopeless, redemption for the renegade and repulsive, love for the unloving and unlovely, kindness for the unkind and unthankful. And all this in full measure and overflowing abundance, because of nothing in the object and because of everything in the Giver, God himself.

And so we can say with Charles Mahaney that 'grace is God's mysterious ongoing acceptance of me whatever my successes or failures'.

One of the greatest secrets of Christian living is to think of grace, walk in grace, breathe grace and, yes, swim into grace. Read this meditation of mine based on Ezekiel 47:1–5.

Walk into grace;
Splash in the sunlit shallows,
Feel fresh the soft wet sand of joy and peace;
Walk into grace.

Wade into grace;
The lurid esplanade of sense declines,
The fast-fry thrill of flesh subsides,
Push through the undertow of sin;
Wade into grace.

Swim into grace;
Cross-currents swirl and swerve your course
Launch out in freedom, strike out strong in truth,

Reflected light marks out the former shore,
But rays from heaven's horizon gild your sea;
Rise in the swell with faith's pure buoyancy,
Supported by the Christ's atlantic love;
Swim into grace.

And so to the meditation. We change the original words very slightly to enable the breathing pattern to be regular:

My grace—is all—you need
My power—perfected—in weakness

Part of the mystery of grace is that we may not feel different after the meditation is over. But just as God's grace has been at work as the prime mover in salvation so now his grace continues to work in very practical ways but this only becomes apparent when we most need it. 'I believe that God will give us all the strength we need to help us resist in times of distress,' says Dietrich Bonhoeffer. 'But he never gives it in advance, lest we should rely on ourselves and not on him alone.'

And so there is no need to feel guilty about our weakness, and it is not necessary to apologize for it. It is, actually, an essential part of the working of God's grace. It's the condition which allows grace most fully to be operative. So we accept our weaknesses. In fact, like St Paul, we may even learn to glory in them, as long as God's grace is revealed through them.

If you find the remaining part of this section misleading please leave it on one side, but it may be helpful for some people to understand the 'spiritual counterpoint' experience that sometimes occurs in meditation. In fact, it could easily happen during the use of this grace prayer phrase. While you are meditating, using the prayer phrase within your own consciousness, you may find faces and situations also arising in your mind where there is a need for God's grace to be revealed. It's as though two melodies are playing through your mind at the same time but there is a creative harmony between them. So don't suppress the second one for it is true intercession. The same counterpoint experience comes when we are using the meditations in the 'healing and wholeness' section.

I believe this is of great value as it not only shows that the basic meditation is firmly established in our minds, but also means that, through the working of the subconscious mind, we are sharing this meditation with other people and radiating out God's grace and healing light in their direction.

The divine potter

The biblical background to this meditation is found in Jeremiah 18:1–6 and as we use it we shall need the help of our imaginations to picture the beautiful, sensitive hands of the divine potter at work, not outside but within us. I wonder if some of you recall the 'Interlude' on 1950s BBC television. In those days programme timings were not so exact as today and—at least twice an evening—a five-minute interlude was programmed to help the schedule. I remember one with waves constantly crashing on a beach, but my favourite showed a potter at work with his wheel. As it revolved, the true craftsman's hands shaped the clay until the vase was complete and ready for firing.

Part of the preparation for the meditation, as we centre down, is to read the Jeremiah passage and then, right from the start, begin to feel the divine hands at work shaping us inwardly into the image of Christ. We know that there will be many parts of our personalities that need reshaping, blemishes of character that must be smoothed off, and that this is often a very long process and, at times, painful. But just as the clay is pliable to the potter's touch, so we, as living clay, gladly surrender to the divine potter. We allow him to create the perfect shape so that we can represent Christ in that right place for us within the body of Christ and in his service to the world. 'Christ has no body now on earth but yours,' said St Teresa of Avila. Herbert Jordan has taken those words as the inspiration for his poem, 'No Body Now':

No hands have I to break the loaves and take
Forgotten multitudes their 'daily bread',
No hands to bless, as once beside the lake,
The 'little ones' from stern disciples fled.

No feet to find the foolish and misled,
Or walk the wards of weariness and pain
No feet with my Samaritan to tread
The lonely road to Jericho again.

No voice to bear my witness to the truth
That sets the shackled man and nation free,
No voice to bring to disillusioned youth
The message that was lived in Galilee.

No body now to serve another's need
And help to batter down dividing doors,
To break the bars of colour, class and creed,
No body now have I on earth—but yours.

In the meditation proper I am using the first verse of a hymn that is well known in some quarters. Although the words are not biblical, in this case the backcloth to the words is straight from Jeremiah 18:1–6.

Have your own way, Lord,
Have your own way;
You are the potter,
I am the clay.
Make me and mould me
After your will;
While I am waiting,
Yielded and still.

A.A. Pollard

With the mental picture of the potter's hands at work within our lives we can make the second half of the verse into the prayer phrase with which we are to live for between fifteen and twenty minutes. The breathing pattern is not straightforward and it is best to experiment with your own, or abandon it altogether if it gets in the way of true meditation. However, it is possible to attempt it in this way:

> Make me—and mould me
> After—your will;
> While I—am waiting
> Yielded—and still

The final words 'waiting, yielded and still' pick up key attitudes that are common to all meditation and the actual regular repetition of them gives one of the most effective centring-down exercises and is recommended.

Returning and resting

The biblical text for this meditation is Isaiah 30:15 which I shall use in the form:

In returning and rest you will be saved;
In quiet trust shall be your strength.

Behind these words are the essentials of salvation. It is possible that Isaiah received this message from God at a time of great national danger. The Assyrian army, with all its barbaric savagery and fearsome weapons of destruction, may well have been threatening Jerusalem. And then, supernaturally, as good King Hezekiah accepted these words as from the Lord and trusted them, the horrifying danger melted away. Possibly some internal problem at home led to the recall of the Assyrian army. But, however it happened, God was in control of the situation and pulling the strings of world events behind the scene.

'In returning' means a radical reappraisal of life and a definite turning away from the old life and to the living God. It is the action of repentance which is not just a light, emotional change of mood but a clear act of will which turns our life through 180 degrees. It's a spiritual right-about-turn. That is the start but it needs to be completed by the act of 'resting'. For us, as Christians, this means going back to all that Christ has done for us and resting in his finished work—cross, resurrection and heavenly reign. And the result is salvation. 'In returning and resting you will be saved', this is God's promise. And so, using Isaiah's words in a full Christian sense, we could say that the first part of the meditation is Christ-centred as it reveals the truth of salvation, and that the second part of it takes us into the area of sanctification in the Holy Spirit:

In quiet trust shall be your strength.

The Holy Spirit himself is the giver of life and power. In his strength alone are we enabled to live a Christian life. Just as the Holy Spirit fills us as we accept Christ as Saviour and Lord, so by 'quiet trust' we live in the Holy Spirit day by day and enable him to express Jesus to the world through us.

The breathing pattern here is a little complicated if we use the full biblical words:

In—returning—and rest—you will—be saved
In—quiet—trust—shall be—your strength

Personally, I find it satisfying to reduce this prayer phrase to its key words, to give them great emphasis and to discover that the meaning and the effect are in no way diminished:

Return—Rest—Saved
Quiet—Trust—Strength

There is a full breath on each word and clearly the slower the words are said the better.

For our centring-down thought, we use Psalm 23, where King David looks back over his life and sees how he learnt to return to the Lord, to rest in him and to walk in his presence and trust his strength.

The Lord is my shepherd; I lack for nothing.
He makes me lie down in green pastures, he
*   leads me to water where I may rest;*
he revives my spirit; for his name's sake he
*   guides me in the right paths.*
Even were I to walk through a valley of
*   deepest darkness I should fear no harm, for*
*   you are with me; your shepherd's staff and*
*   crook afford me comfort.*
You spread a table for me in the presence of
*   my enemies; you have richly anointed my*
*   head with oil, and my cup brims over.*
Goodness and love unfailing will follow me all
*   the days of my life, and I shall dwell in the*
*   house of the Lord throughout the years to*
*   come.*

PSALM 23 (REB)

My God supplies

*My God will supply every need of yours
according to his riches in glory in Christ Jesus.*

PHILIPPIANS 4:19

There are a number of reasons for believing that
the church at Philippi stood foremost in St Paul's
affection. No church, then or now, is without its
problems and Paul clearly alludes to a need for
greater unity amongst the Christian fellowship
there and he also singles out two or three individuals who need to mend their ways. But as he
wrote his letter from his position of house arrest
in Rome his heart would have gone out to Lydia,
and the Roman gaoler and his family whom Paul
had baptized in the middle of the night, the
young girl who had been healed of a spirit of div-
ination, and others. He knew he was writing to
people who loved him and who had proved so
generous in their faith. It had been their joy to
share with other Christians over and above what
they could really afford. The generosity of God
had so thrilled them that there was no way they
could hold back from giving out to others.

And so Paul gives them this glorious promise straight from the Lord. He says that we can never out-give our generous God because he will give back out of all the glorious resources that are to be found in Christ Jesus. The reigning Lord is a giving Lord and he channels his munificence through the Holy Spirit as he moves into every corner of the earth.

Inevitably, we shall find items of need arising in our minds as we meditate. Of course, these needs may be so great that they press in on us constantly. This meditation is meant to be superimposed over the problems of which we are conscious. This is God's word, his answer. We don't know how he will be working his sovereign will out for us but we affirm that he, the living God, is moving into our life-situation to change circumstances and supply needs in ways which he decides.

The meditation breaks down into four lines of three words each, and the breathing rhythm is straightforward:

My—God—supplies
All—your—needs
From—glorious—riches
In—Christ—Jesus

The consciousness of great needs tends to create stress within us and so the centring-down process is especially important before we start revolving the prayer phrase.

Begin by using part of the poem 'Dear Lord and Father of mankind'. Jesus himself knew the secret of becoming still before fully entering into prayer. He went out very early in the morning onto the Galilean hillside to be quiet with his heavenly Father. The wet dew of the grass was the outward symbol of the dew of the Spirit that immediately began to refresh his own soul.

O Sabbath rest by Galilee!
O calm of hills above,
Where Jesus knelt to share with thee
The silence of eternity,
Interpreted by love!

With that deep hush subduing all
Our words and works that drown
The tender whisper of thy call,
As noiseless let thy blessing fall
As fell the manna down.

Drop thy still dews of quietness,
Till all our strivings cease;
Take from our souls the strain and stress
And let our ordered lives confess
The beauty of thy peace.

Breathe through the heats of our desire
Thy coolness and thy balm;
Let sense be dumb, let flesh retire;
Speak through the earthquake, wind and fire,
O still small voice of calm!

John Greenleaf Whittier

My only real need, each day, is to know God. The very purpose of life is to arise out of all personal conflict, disturbance, worry and fear to recognise only God. I have to learn, patiently, each day to know that his grace is sufficient for everything in my life. I need to know that God possesses all these glorious riches which I need in Christ and that he wants to share them with me.

This day I am centred in him, and his peace, therefore, fills the whole range of my being. This day I dwell in the security of the Kingdom of God where God is able to meet all my needs from his glorious riches in Christ Jesus.

Brother Mandus

The Lord's Prayer

Although this is strictly intercession rather than meditation, it is possible to use the Lord's Prayer very effectively as a meditation-intercession. In fact, because we usually say it too quickly its real meaning may break through to us again if we use it rather more slowly. We shall separate it into clauses of three words each and they can be repeated for an almost unlimited period as more of their meaning and application become clear. Only the briefest words of explanation are provided here but quiet repetition allows the Holy Spirit to reveal situations which need prayer. It's worth recalling that as this is the only prayer which Jesus gave to his followers it must possess unique value and power.

Abba, Father, God: Savour again the privilege of addressing God as 'Abba'. If Jesus had revealed no other truth about God to us than this it would have still been truly revolutionary.

Your name hallowed: God's name reveals his true character so it should always be deeply reverenced and made holy.

Your reign come: everywhere, but especially in those places which are flashing into my mind at this moment. Your reign is Christ's reign and we affirm his kingship everywhere.

Your will done: as in heaven, so on earth and especially may the Church of Christ be his instrument in revealing and implementing God's will. May every member of the body of Christ be sensitive to the mind of Christ.

Grant daily bread: our prayer is for physical bread to reach all in need. But also, knowing that we cannot live by physical bread alone, we pray for spiritual food daily.

Cleanse our sin: the sin of falling short of God's standards, the sin of deviating from his path of life, the sin of breaking his laws. We try to identify everything in our lives that is not true to Christ's mind and way and which wounds God's heart of love.

As we forgive: the great condition of living within God's acceptance and forgiveness is that we show our appreciation of it by passing it on to others.

Lead us Lord: lead us and guide us into your ways which are righteousness and peace. May we trust you fully and not stray into the place of danger where we begin to trust ourselves.

Deliver from evil: deliver us from every attack of our spiritual enemy. We bind him in the name of Jesus and command him to get behind us today and never to touch us, and our loved ones, in body, mind or spirit.

Kingdom, power, glory: as our prayer began with the hallowing of God's holy name, so it ends with a doxology to his glory. He is the Alpha and the Omega, so we begin and end in adoration and worship. To him be all the glory for ever.

The same breathing pattern can be maintained throughout this prayer-meditation: one breath on each of the three words in each section. Don't be surprised if it revolutionizes your praying. You may be amazed, one day, to discover that an hour has flashed past while you are using it.

The divine Creator

This is the 'green' meditation in the sense that it expresses the delight that we are meant to share with God in his creative activity. A good preparation for this meditation would be to read through Genesis 1 and feel again the joy of God in seeing how good was his creation—'and God saw that it was good'. And then read Proverbs 8:22–31 as a divine commentary on it.

St John's first letter makes the two ultimate statements about God: God is light; God is love. And Jesus himself revealed that he was the light of the world. And so the meditation is Trinitarian as we sense the binding joy of the Spirit as he also rejoices with the Father and the Son in their triune creative activity.

God—is—love
Christ—is—light
Spirit—is—joy

The breathing pattern is straightforward. We just need to treat 'Spirit' as a monosyllable.

The centring-down introduction could include this poem which is entitled, 'In the beginning...'.

God laughed,
And the firmament fumed and spluttered with
   pleasure;
And the sea shook the foam of his hair from
   his eyes;
And earth was glad.

The sound of the laughter
Was like the swaying and swinging of thunder
   in mirth;
Like the rush of the north on a drowsy and
   dozing land;
It was cool. It was clear.

The lion leapt down
At the bleating feet of the frightened lamb and
   smiled;
And the viper was tamed by the thrill of the
   earth,
At the holy laughter.

We laughed,
For the Lord was laughing with us in the
   evening;
For the laughter of love went pealing into the
   night;
And it was good.

Paul Bunday

Maranatha

What a wealth of spiritual longing is concentrated in this prayer. If ever a prayer was 'Spirit borne' to the throne of grace it is this. The words come from 1 Corinthians 16:22 and represent one of the earliest prayers of the Church, where the original Aramaic of Jewish Christians is remembered and reproduced. The cry has continued to be heard all down the Christian centuries for it catches the intense longing for the risen, glorified Lord to appear now amongst his people in mercy and grace, and at the end of time in glory. 'Come, Lord Jesus!' Come soon; come now!

This prayer phrase is very popular at the present moment and thousands meditate on it daily. If you are side-tracked by wandering thoughts gently pull yourself back on course. Alternatively, observe where that straying thought has led you and then let your cry ascend for that person or situation. Allow the counterpoint of intercession to weave in and out of your meditation.

The prayer phrase is broken into four syllables:

As you breath in meditation you may be conscious of the Holy Spirit praying through you, for this is not only the great cry of the Church but of the Holy Spirit himself.

As we begin to centre down take the words of Meister Eckhart: 'God is bound to act, to pour himself into thee as soon as he shall find thee ready.'

The meditation depends on a sense of rising expectancy moving within us, a new vision of God always coming to meet us, always bigger than our problem. Isaac Watts has this vision in one of his hymns:

The mighty God, whose matchless power
is ever new and ever young,
and firm endures, while endless years
their everlasting circles run.

We prepare for the quiet repetition of:

Maranatha

We centre down with Edward Shillito's poem that welcomes God's life breaking into ours:

Away with gloom, away with doubt,
with all the morning stars we sing;
with all the sons of God we shout
the praises of a King,
Alleluia, alleluia,
of our returning King.

Away with death, and welcome life;
in him we died and live again:
and welcome peace, away with strife,
for he returns to reign.
Alleluia, alleluia,
the Crucified shall reign.

Then welcome beauty, he is fair;
and welcome youth, for he is young;
and welcome spring; and everywhere
let merry songs be sung,
Alleluia, alleluia,
for such a King be sung.

Edward Shillito, by permission
of Oxford University Press

Come to me

This meditation is based on the actual words of Jesus and the truth which flows from them. It begins with his gracious invitation to all who are stressed, depressed and heavy laden to come to him. And behind those words lie the promise which he gives in John 6:37 that those who come to him will never be cast out. The invitation is warm and compelling: 'Come to me, all who labour and are heavy laden, and I will give you rest. Take my yoke upon you, and learn from me; for I am gentle and lowly in heart, and you will find rest for your souls' (Matthew 11:28–29).

Secondly, we move to Jesus' great affirmation in John 14:6: 'I am the way, and the truth, and the life.' He is saying to us that he is the way through life when we respond to his invitation to come to him and follow him. There is so much we need to learn, many problems to solve, many dangers to overcome. But the simple act of faith in following him, day by day, is the secret of walking with him in his way.

In simple trust, like those who heard
Beside the Syrian sea,

The gracious calling of the Lord.
Let us, like them, without a word
Rise up and follow thee.

John Greenleaf Whittier

He is also the truth, the ultimate truth about God and about life itself. When God wanted to reveal his final truth to us he did not shout great philosophical statements down from heaven, he did not write unmistakable words in the sky, but he sent a man who embodied his truth in daily living and redemptive dying. Jesus is the Word of God and so the final truth.

And then again, Jesus is life itself. We are permitted to share in his resurrection life, his abundant life. Those who come to him are certainly not cast out, rather they gloriously share his eternal life—the greatest gift of all.

Finally, this meditation is summed up in the words of St Paul: 'We have the mind of Christ' (1 Corinthians 2:16). The mind of Jesus permeates our human mind so that his thoughts, his reactions, his decisions become implanted in our minds. How we need to become sensitive to his thoughts, and meditation will help us to live in his mind. The full prayer phrase becomes:

Come—to—me
Way—Truth—Life
Mind—of—Christ

As you can see, the breathing rhythm is perfectly regular. However, before using these simple, profound words the centring-down procedure is vitally important. Here I am giving several meditative passages based on scripture which prepare the ground. The author is unknown.

God is love and he who dwells in love dwells in God and God in him. Love creates perfect harmony, perfect well-being. Love is the fulfilling of the law, it satisfies all requirements and fulfils all conditions. Love is perfect adjustment to life, perfect reconciliation to God's will. Love is, therefore, the healing power. In love there is no resentment, no fear, no pride, no fault-finding, no possessiveness, no jealousy, no envy, no selfishness. Love is forgiveness, generosity, humility, forbearance, understanding, compassion. Love is Christ-like. Jesus is the spirit of perfect love. Love is God's gift. The love of God is shed abroad in our hearts. Herein is love, not that we love... but that God loved us.

I have been crucified with Christ, nevertheless I live, yet not I but Christ lives in me; and the life which I now live in the flesh I live by faith in the Son of God, who loved me and gave himself for me.

Christ in me is perfect peace.
Christ in me is perfect faith.
Christ in me is perfect joy.
Christ in me is abundant life.

Therefore I do not hesitate to come to him—which is where the prayer phrase begins.

I can't but you can

The angel revealed to Mary at the annunciation that God's promises can never fail and that nothing is impossible for him. The words above are not strictly biblical but they sum up the angel's words to Mary and other passages such as: 'All authority in heaven and on earth has been given to me' (Matthew 28:18). They affirm that Christ's resurrection power is available to all believers and that God's power is always greater than our problem. The Holy Spirit is always at work within us and the risen Lord is also always interceding for us at the right hand of the Father. 'I can do all things in [Christ], who strengthens me' (Philippians 4:13). But it must be through Christ, which means that we must first be 'in him'.

Here we don't try to hide our weaknesses, problems or failures but rather set them against God's power, the power that was at work raising Jesus from the dead. In Christ we are brought into that stream of resurrection power.

The breathing pattern is very important here. We need one full breath on 'I can't'. In fact, it doesn't matter if we breathe rather quickly at this point to represent the fact of our weakness—almost amounting to panic. This then contrasts with the slow full breath for each word of 'But—you—can'. Our God reigns. He is sufficient for all our need. So he is worthy to receive all honour and glory and worship.

As we centre down for this meditation we need to learn to live in the risen power of Christ. We have been raised with him so his resurrection power is always at work within us. We need to allow ourselves to be Spirit borne, which means abiding in the centre of his elevating power.

Bless the Lord, my soul;
with all my being I bless his holy name.
Bless the Lord, my soul,
and forget none of his benefits.
He pardons all my wrongdoing
and heals all my ills.
He rescues me from death's pit
and crowns me with love and compassion.
He satisfies me with all good in the prime of life,
and my youth is renewed like an eagle's.

PSALM 103:1–5 (REB)

The Lord your God is in your midst,
a warrior who will keep you safe.
He will rejoice over you and be glad;
he will show his love once more;
he will exult over you with a shout of joy
as on a festal day.

ZEPHANIAH 3:17 (REB)

Late that same day, the first day of the week,
when the disciples were together behind locked
doors for fear of the Jews, Jesus came and
stood among them. 'Peace be with you!' he said.

JOHN 20:19 (REB)

Jesus is still moving through locked doors,
locked minds and barred hearts:

By this time they had reached the village to
which they were going, and he made as if to
continue his journey. But they pressed him: 'Stay
with us, for evening approaches, and the day is
almost over.' So he went in to stay with them.
And when he had sat down with them at table,
he took bread and said the blessing; he broke the
bread, and offered it to them. Then their eyes
were opened, and they recognized him; but he
vanished from their sight. They said to one
another, 'Were not our hearts on fire as he talked
with us on the road and explained the scriptures
to us?'

LUKE 24:28–32 (REB)

Jesus still meets us as bread is broken in his
name and as the Word of God is opened by the
Spirit:

Lo, Jesus meets us, risen from the tomb!
Lovingly he greets us, scatters fear and gloom;
Let the church with gladness hymns of
     triumph sing,

For her Lord now liveth, death hast lost its
  sting.

No more we doubt thee, glorious Prince of life;
Life is nought without thee: aid us in our
  strife;
Make us more than conquerors, through thy
  deathless love:
Bring us safe through Jordan to thy home
  above.

Thine be the glory, risen conquering Son,
Endless is the vict'ry thou o'er death hast
  won!

E.L. Budry, translated by R.B. Hoyle

Jesus, my all in all thou art,
My rest in toil, my ease in pain,
The medicine of my broken heart,
In war my peace, in loss my gain,
My smile beneath the tyrant's frown,
In shame my glory and my crown.

In want my plentiful supply,
In weakness my almighty power,
In bonds my perfect liberty,
My light in Satan's darkest hour,
In grief my joy unspeakable,
My life in death, my heaven in hell.

Charles Wesley

I can't—but—you—can

Meditation in the heavenlies

Once again we are using words in this meditation which contain a wealth of meaning. The title indicates that we are moving into the realm of the ascended Lord. We may well put the question, 'What is Jesus Christ actually doing at this moment?' And the answer is revealed to us in the New Testament through the letters of St Paul, the author of Hebrews and through St John's first letter and the book of Revelation. The short answer is that he is applying his blood, he is making intercession and he is proclaiming his name.

There is a sense in which we could say that the ascension was the greatest of all Christ's mighty acts for it is the climax and summation of the incarnation, the cross and the resurrection. Because of Jesus' ascension we now have a man in heaven, a friend in high places. When Jesus died on the cross the atoning value of his blood was not only that it was shed physically but, more importantly, was offered in the very holy of holies in the heavenly place. In fact, the letter to the Hebrews does not speak of the resurrection at all. The blood shed on Calvary is immediately offered in the heavenlies indicating the power and universality of the atonement. It's as though Jesus passed straight from the cross into his ascended state.

When St John says that 'the blood of Jesus... cleanses us from all sin' (1 John 1:7) he is thinking of Jesus' heavenly ministry which continues to the end of time as he applies his blood to human need bringing peace, forgiveness, restoration and reconciliation. And he does this through his constant intercession.

Romans 8:34 and Hebrews 7:25 confirm this continuing act of prayer which always radiates out from the heavenly throne of grace. Because Jesus is the same 'yesterday and today and for ever' (Hebrews 13:8), his intercession now must be the same as his intercession during his ministry and must be true to his character and words which were revealed through the Gospel record. What an amazing and breath-catching thought that Jesus Christ is praying for us continually to bring our life and circumstances into conformity with his will.

Finally, we turn to the name of Jesus before whom every knee must bow (Philippians 2:5–11). As it is the name now of our ascended Lord, it is the name of grace and victory, of love and power. It has a unique value, for no foreign body or dark power can stand before it. It is the name of wholeness, life, peace and hope. In one title it sums up all that Jesus is and accomplished. No wonder Charles Wesley affirmed:

Jesus! the name high over all,
In hell or earth or sky;
Angels and men before it fall,
And devils fear and fly.

Come then to the very throne room of heaven as we prepare ourselves for this profound act of meditation by using the words of Charitie Lees Bancroft:

Before the throne of God above
I have a strong, a perfect plea:
A great High Priest, whose name is Love,
Who ever lives and pleads for me.

My name is graven on his hands,
My name is written on his heart;
I know that while in heaven he stands
No tongue can bid me thence depart.

When Satan tempts me to despair,
And tells me of the guilt within,
Upward I look, and see him there
Who made an end of all my sin.

Because the sinless Saviour died,
My sinful soul is counted free;
For God, the Just, is satisfied
To look on him and pardon me.

Behold him there! the risen Lamb!
My perfect, spotless Righteousness,
The great unchangeable I AM,
The King of glory and of grace!

One with himself, I cannot die;
My soul is purchased by his blood;
My life is hid with Christ on high,
With Christ, my Saviour and my God.

The meditation, again, has a simple breathing pattern:

Blood—of—Jesus
Prayer—of—Jesus
Name—of—Jesus

Our study of meditation began in the dust and dirt, the pressure and strain of daily life, and it ends in the complete harmony, beauty and wholeness of the heavenly realm. As we live in Christ we link the two so that we may glorify God, experience true wholeness in the Spirit and become what we truly are.

If you have enjoyed reading *Spirit Borne*, you may wish to know that BRF produces two regular series of Bible reading notes published three times a year (in January, May and September). *Guidelines* contains commentary and reflection on the Bible, arranged in weekly sections, with a devotional 'Guidelines' section each week. *New Daylight* contains daily readings with printed Bible passages, brief comments and prayers, and is also available in a large print version.

Copies of *Guidelines* and *New Daylight* may be obtained from your local Christian bookshop or by subscription direct from BRF (see over).

For more information about *Guidelines*, *New Daylight* and the full range of BRF publications, write to: The Bible Reading Fellowship, Peter's Way, Sandy Lane West, OXFORD OX4 5HG (Tel. 01865 748227).

SUBSCRIPTION ORDER FORM

Please send me the following, beginning with the Jan/May/Sep* issue:
*delete as appropriate

Qty

_____	Guidelines	£9.00 p.a.†	_____
_____	New Daylight	£9.00 p.a.†	_____
_____	New Daylight large print	£12.00 p.a.†	_____

All prices include postage and packing.

Please complete the payment details below—all orders must be accompanied by the appropriate payment—and send your completed order to **BRF, Peter's Way, Sandy Lane West, Oxford OX4 5HG.**

Name . . . .

Address . . . .

. . . . Postcode . . . .

Signed. . . . . Date . . . .

Payment for subscription(s)   £ _____
Donation   £ _____
Total enclosed   £ _____

Payment by cheque ❑ postal order ❑ Visa ❑ Mastercard ❑

Expiry date of card . . . .

Signature . . . .
(essential if paying by credit card)

BRF is a Reg. Charity (No. 233280)   SB

NB *New Daylight* and *Guidelines* may also be obtained from your local Christian bookshop—ask at your local shop for details.
† Prices quoted are for subscriptions beginning May 1996 issue.